Max and Me

Written and Illustrated by Ethan Love

NENGE BOOKS

Max and Me

Written & Illustrated by Ethan Love

Desktop layout by Nenge Books

Copyright © Ethan Clifford Love 2018

All rights reserved. No part of this book may be reproduced, distributed, or transmitted in any form or by any means, including photocopying, recording, or other electronic or mechanical methods, without the prior written permission from the publisher, except in the case of brief quotations embodied in a book review and certain other noncommercial uses permitted by the Australian Copyright Act 1968. The Act allows a maximum of one chapter or 10% of this book, whichever is the greater to be photocopied by any educational institution for its educational purposes provided that the educational institution (or body that administers it) has given a remuneration notice to the Copyright Agency Limited (CAL).

Published by Nenge Books, Australia, June 2018
ABN 26809396184
Email: nengebooks1@gmail.com
www.nengebooks.com

This book is available from the publisher or by order through bookshops. Nenge Books uses print-on-demand technology to publish small to medium quantities of quality books assisting independent authors to publish their works cost effectively.

This is Ethan's first book, written and illustrated aged 8 years old.

ISBN 978-0-6480675-7-3

For my family to remember Max.

The people and animals in this book are real. The story is true, everything actually happened.

Once upon a time

there was a dog...

... a dog called Max.

He was a friendly dog

and liked to sit in the sun.

Max lived with his mum, dad

and sister called Molly.

One day Max's mum had a baby.

She called him Ethan (that's me).

One year later Max and Ethan's mum

had another baby.

She called him Ryan.

I grew up having Max

and Ryan grew up having Molly.

Max and me had the best adventures together, like walking around the block, going to the oval and other stuff like that...

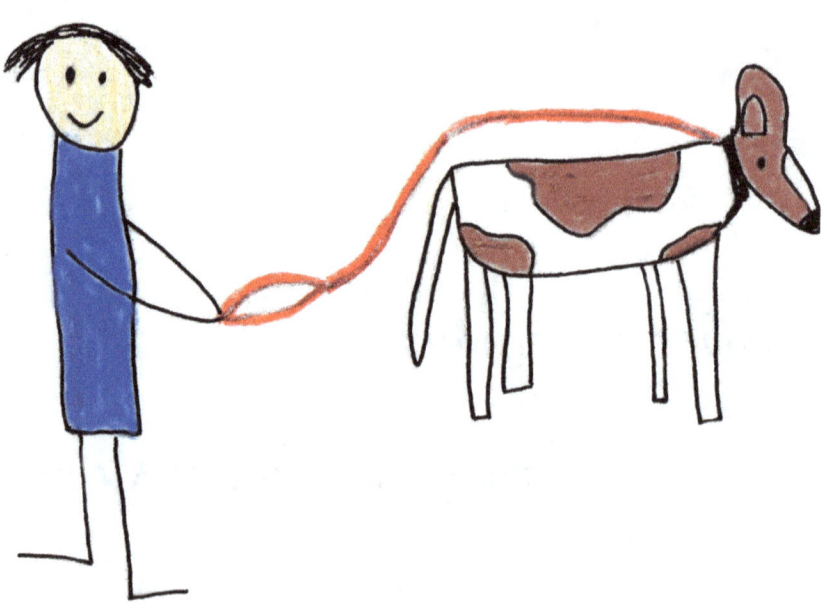

...with Daddy of course!

Sometimes we walked them

to school...

... everyone loved them.

When we took him to the oval.

He liked to run across it with us

and chase all the rabbits.

But he never caught one

even though he could run really fast!

When we went around the block

he always pulled, but sometimes he didn't.

His favourite food was cicadas and

he liked licking little red berries

off the ground.

Then when I was 8

Judah was born as a baby.

But when Judah was 3 months old

Max died.

But Judah still got to meet him.

We were all sad

and crying

because we loved Max.

So now we only have Molly.

Because Max is not here

we give Molly lots of hugs.

And that's how it is until Molly dies.

After that we might get a cat.

Max was my friend and

I will always miss him.

Max and Molly when they were puppies in 2008.

Me as a baby with Max and Molly in 2010.

Me, Judah, Max (back), Molly and Ryan, 6th March 2018.

Walking Max and Molly to school, 7th March 2018.

Max

21.10.2008 – 9.3.2018

www.ingramcontent.com/pod-product-compliance
Lightning Source LLC
Chambersburg PA
CBHW072116290426
44110CB00014B/1936